# From
# One Loneliness
# to
# Another

*Urdu Poems By:*
*Hamid Yazdani*

*Translated By:*
*M. Salim-ur- Rahman*

*Copyright*

*Published in 2022 by Green Zone Publishing*
*A division of Dr. Sohail MPC Inc.*
*213 Byron St. South*
*Whitby, Ontario Canada L1N 4P7*
*T. 905- 666-7253, F. 905-666-4397*
*E-mail: welcome@drsohail.com*
*Website: www.drsohail.com*

*From One Loneliness to Another: Yazdani, Hamid*
*Translated by: M. Salim-ur- Rahman*

*ISBN: 978-1-927874-59-2*

| | |
|---|---|
| *Cover Design:* | *Shahid Shafiq* |
| *Cover Design:* | *Uzma Aziz* |
| *Textual Design:* | *Marcelina Naini* |

*For my children*
*Zernaab, Ameed, Areeb, Rabia Yazdani*

*&*

*my grandchildren*
*Ayaan and Uzayr Yazdani*

## Table of Contents

# CREATIVE GIFTS

Translating a poem is like building a creative bridge between two languages and cultures. Salim-ur-Rahman has built wonderful creative bridges between Hamid Yazdani's Urdu poems and his English readers. When we read those translations, we realize how much Hamid Yazdani is fascinated with nature, seasons and time. He introduces us to the magic and mystery of mornings and evenings, days and nights, springs and falls, summers and winters.

Since a poet's success depends upon how much he can help his readers see extra-ordinary in the ordinary, I consider Hamid Yazdani a highly successful poet. Through his poetry he can inspire his readers to see life through his unique eyes.

It is easy to translate prose but very difficult to translate poetry because it deals with images and feelings, similes and metaphors, mysteries and meanings that can easily be lost in the translation but Salim-ur-Rahman has done justice to Hamid Yazdani's poetry. His translations are more than translations, they are rather re-creations of Urdu poems in English capturing the essence and spirit of Hamid Yazdani's poems with all their subtleties. Salim-ur- Rahman has also added his own creativity to the poems to make translations more genuine and authentic.

Let me share one poem that touched me at a deeper level. For years and decades, I have encountered June 21st in my life as it is the longest day of the year. That day is close to my heart and has a special meaning for me as it is very close to my birthday. But I had never experienced it the way Hamid Yazdani presented it in his poem. After reading that poem I developed a new relationship with June 21st and for the rest of my life I will see it with new eyes, hear it with new ears, think about it with a new mind and feel it with a new heart. Hamid Yazdani helped me enjoy, appreciate and admire the magic and mystery of life by helping me experience the extra-ordinary in the ordinary. That makes Hamid Yazdani a successful poet. Now I would like you to read that poem so that you can also have an existential encounter with it.

*JUNE 21st*

*Blood!*
*Lava pouring down a volcano*

*Breath!*
*On fire like the scorching winds*
*in the dead of summer*

*From One Loneliness to Another*

*Dreams!*
*Resemble forlorn, leafless branches.*

*Heart!*
*A furnace in full blaze.*

*Red-hot lead---*
*That's what my hearing has become.*

*Words!*
*They stand for what sunlight's swelter,*
*I don't know.*

*The sky!*
*A stunning melting stillness.*
*The soft stir*
*of tired, worn-out winds.*

*I speak to you, wide open eyes,*
*which look like blisters;*
*no matter what you do,*
*the day would never come to an end,*
*it seems.*

We all experience a night everyday but when we read Hamid Yazdani's poem about night we start experiencing it in a different way. He writes:

*From One Loneliness to Another*

## NIGHT IS A FOOTLOOSE GIRL

*You who travel through*
*a plenitude of light!*
*Night is a footloose girl.*
*Wandering about aimlessly*
*through the unknown streets of time.*
*A few cloudy stars*
*or eyes which stare at her*
*with lust stick to her black jacket.*
*She walks unsteadily*
*in a state of euphoria*
*because she wants*
*to control her hysteria.*
*Meanwhile on the morning's chessboard*
*the checkmate of the moments*
*concealed in the mist*
*now makes itself manifest.*
*Even the thick mist*
*can't hide the gasping wounds.*
*She has gone the round*
*of all the casino seasons*
*in front of the roulette.*
*The night, aimlessly wandering,*

*has lost all her stars*
*and as she lies down*
*to go to sleep,*
*wrapped up in a moonless dark,*
*she holds a half-burnt dream*
*in her fingers; she thinks,*
*lightly puffing away,*
*that surely one day,*
*in the gamble called life,*
*a win will come hurtling her away.*
*Someday this ritual*
*of checkmates will be overturned.*
*Maybe because she has still got*
*a moon in her purse.*
*Look into her purse,*
*traveller!*
*Night is a footloose girl.*

These are just a couple of examples to highlight how Hamid Yazdani's poems change how we relate to our environment and start seeing usual things in an unusual way.

I would like to congratulate Hamid Yazdani for creating such wonderful poems and thank Salim-ur-Rehman for translating them in English so that Hamid Yazdani's Canadian friends can also enjoy his poems as they would not have been able to appreciate them in Urdu. I feel proud to be Hamid Yazdani's friend and feel honoured that he asked me to write a few words about his creative gifts for English speaking readers all over the world. I hope he keeps on writing and inspiring his readers by sharing his knowledge, experience and wisdom in his creations. He is such a gifted, talented and enlightened writer and scholar.

*Dr. Khalid Sohail*
*Whitby, Ontario. Canada*

# *Times*

*From One Loneliness to Another*

*From One Loneliness to Another*

## *A DAY BEGINS*

*A day begins.*
*A vagrant day begins.*
*A vagrant, autumn-like, day begins.*
*The rotting leaves of the maple,*
*lying here and there on the lawn,*
*open their fists.*
*Who knows what language they speak*
*and what they say!*
*I know only this much*
*that when life's sun is on its way down*
*and the light mellows,*
*even the dust of memories*
*turns into gold.*
*I wander about for hours,*
*my eyes replete with this gold,*
*by the lakes which conceal themselves*
*in gray mist,*
*on the rolling hills*
*of a yesterday.*
*Only taking a single day*
*along with me*

*From One Loneliness to Another*

*and a night which dies down*
*as I breathe.*

*I have no idea when*
*this, now bright now dark, door*
*to the past swung open.*

*And a day begins.*

## *A HOPE*

*The autumn's message*
*set out on the maple leaves.*
*Whose eyes are these*
*sprouting forth from*
*the sidewalk's dry grass?*

*Whose heart would it please*
*this somewhat colourless season*
*blossoming out of a fevered palm?*

*One of these days*
*the April, redolent*
*with your memories*
*will come around again.*

## DURING A SQUARISH NIGHT

*We have fashioned words*
*out of sunlight.*
*Even so the darkness keeps*
*spreading across the page.*
*The wilting look of words*
*as they cling to the crumbling walls.*
*The shadowy figures wandering*
*deep inside the chat rooms*
*long to touch the statue of a dream*
*imprisoned in moments,*
*an entanglement of road*
*or altercations in the Tea House?*

*A concourse of lights.*
*Even so the wounds*
*look like dark spaces.*
*The scene, shattered*
*into ripples, merging*
*with evening, keeps*
*coming into prominence*
*within the squarish night.*
*The paper keeps*
*getting darker and darker.*

*From One Loneliness to Another*

# FIRST POEM OF THE YEAR

*A new year appears*
*on the horizon again*
*and once again*
*misted over path of memories.*

*A few reflections, a few names*
*swathed in the haze.*
*In the eyes of an errant dawn*
 *the shattered dreams*
*of yesterday.*

*And the new morning*
*is about to receive as its lot*
*the accumulation of the misgivings*
*that belonged to the night*
*which is gone,*
*and all the holdings which constitute*
*a respite for sorrows.*

*Once more the insensate remoteness*
*of a few familiar moments*
*dissolves in my breathing.*

*From One Loneliness to Another*

*And the New Year's window*
*begins to open*
*on the rank and ravaged lawn*
*of the day that has departed.*

*A new year appears*
*on the horizon again*
*and once again*
*misted over path of memories.*

## IN AN ALMOST EMPTY CAFÉTERIA

*An evening coming down the stairs,*
*avoiding even its own shadow,*
*touching the green branches,*
*awakening bewilderment*
*after bewilderment which adhere*
*to the grimy chairs.*

*At a little distance*
*a coffee maker spewing out a bitter, black night.*
*A darkness spilling out*
*from a clean, transparent cup.*
*Turning into steam*
*life clings to the ceiling.*

*A few soft sounds*
*dozing at a table.*
*A somewhat indifferent,*
*rather murky light.*
*Smoke rises from the ashtray,*
*reflecting mirror by mirror,*
*a meeting with hardly*
*any warmth left in it.*

*From One Loneliness to Another*

*The moon, the clouds, the trees,*
*the hedges, the pathway*
*and the trailing red plants*
 *entangled in each other…*

*A season locked up*
*in a glasshouse, so to say.*

*Listen, heartbeats! Keep quiet.*

*See the grimy evening*
*as it comes down the gray stairs,*
*withdrawn into itself,*
*touching the green branches;*
*just because of a slight*
*stir you make*
*or a faint rustle,*
*you may frighten her,*
*causing it to turn back.*

*Don't let it happen!*

*This evening and the girls*
*a little like evening themselves.*

# *JUNE 21ˢᵗ*

*Blood!*
*Lava pouring down a volcano*

*Breath!*
*On fire like the scorching winds*
*in the dead of summer*

*Dreams!*
*Resemble forlorn, leafless branches.*

*Heart!*
*A furnace in full blaze.*

*Red-hot lead---*
*That's what my hearing has become.*

*Words!*
*They stand for what sunlight's swelter,*
*I don't know.*

*The sky!*

*A stunning melting stillness.*

*From One Loneliness to Another*

*The soft stir*
*of tired, worn-out winds.*

*I speak to you, wide open eyes,*
*which look like blisters;*
*no matter what you do,*
*the day would never come to an end,*
*it seems.*

## NEW YEAR'S EVE

*A night somewhat like a tree.*
*A night, entangled branch by branch,*
*in lonesome stars.*
*A night somewhat like a tree.*

*In the courtyard of dark time*
*pledges and promises*
*drift about among dry leaves.*

*Whispers which belong to wet moments.*
*Demolished soft sounds.*
*The indifference of pale bodies.*
*Windows of pain.*
*Stairs of hurt.*
*The shaking edifice of desires.*
*Like a chill shadow*
*on the night's floor*
*the wind roaming about*
*on the dark floor,*
*tramples on the dream,*
*cuts up the moon,*

*From One Loneliness to Another*

*mocks the hoary water.*
*There are clouds, there is snow*
*An old, tattered, dusty carpet.*
*Memory is a carpet.*
*Who is going to attend this feast?*
*I wonder.*

*The wind which blows in*
*like a season never observed before?*
*Who is going to attend this feast?*

*Who is going to attend*
*the first feast of grief?*
*I wonder.*

## NIGHT IS A FOOTLOOSE GIRL

*You who travel through*
*a plenitude of light!*

*Night is a footloose girl.*
*Wandering about aimlessly*
*through the unknown streets of time.*

*A few cloudy stars*
*or eyes which stare at her*
*with lust stick to her black jacket.*

*She walks unsteadily*
*in a state of euphoria*
*because she wants*
*to control her hysteria.*

*Meanwhile on the morning's chessboard*
*the checkmate of the moments*
*concealed in the mist*
*now makes itself manifest.*

*Even the thick mist*
*can't hide the gasping wounds.*

*From One Loneliness to Another*

*She has gone the round*
*of all the casino seasons*
*in front of the roulette.*

*The night, aimlessly wandering,*
*has lost all her stars*
*and as she lies down*
*to go to sleep,*
*wrapped up in a moonless dark,*
*she holds a half-burnt dream*
*in her fingers; she thinks,*
*lightly puffing away,*
*that surely one day,*
*in the gamble called life,*
*a win will come hurtling her way.*

*Someday this ritual*
*of checkmates will be overturned.*
*Maybe because she has still got*
*a moon in her purse.*
*Look into her purse,*
*traveller!*

*Night is a footloose girl.*

*From One Loneliness to Another*

# *OCTOBER*

*This early shower in autumn*
*would transform birds*
*into poems from dawn to dusk*
*on faded leaves.*

## *ON THE ULTIMATE SHORE*

*Desires which hold on tightly*
*to the fiery hues of autumn*
*or a handful of dreams*
*entangled in the moonlight's hedge.*

*The illusion of a shadow*
*across the path of a dying breath.*
*The sound as the last dry leaf*
*falls on the shining floor of silence.*

*Only a rustling sound*
*in the somewhat murky light,*
*and the heat of smoke*
*beyond the rustling sound,*
*like a sky aglow.*

## *SPRING*

*What has happened?*
*Is spring here?*
*The dream of my artistry,*
*which is like a wound,*
*opens; and the vision*
*is on fire again.*

*Memory is lit up.*
*This time round*
*memory is lit up*
*in such a manner somehow,*
*even the dark corners*
*of the house shine brightly.*

*The seasons which had come*
*to a standstill in my album*
*have heard of it.*
*Who has placed a flower*
*as an embellishment,*
*on your scented portrait in red?*

*Reaching out from*
*a burnt out dream,*

*why has the creeper, as it descends*
*from the marble cornice,*
*come up to the table,*
*by passing the glowing fireplace?*

*Who stole the dream*
*placed within a rosy tale?*
*Who has steeped the mirror*
*of my words in autumnal hues?*

*The balmy seasons*
*which had come to a standstill*
*in my album*
*have heard of it.*
*Time, hunched among*
*the green branches,*
*has nothing to say.*

*What has happened?*
*Is spring here?*
*The dream of my artistry,*
*which is like a wound,*
*opens; and everyone's vision*
*is on fire again.*

*From One Loneliness to Another*

# THE FIRST DAY OF A NEW MILLENIUM

*This day also comes,*
*rises one might say,*
*from the newspaper,*
*exactly like so many*
*other ordinary days.*
*Say, how many crows*
*sat on the cow's head?*
*The cow doesn't know how to count.*
*The cobbler goes on mending*
*the same slipper.*
*The whole crowd,*
*which has set its sights*
*on stale pieces of meat.*
*Flies, customers.*
*A shabby, sickly dog.*
*Each of them driven*
*by hunger.*
*The feebleness of lives*
*which have been smashed to smithereens.*
*In which direction*
*do the drains run?*

*From One Loneliness to Another*

*The light keeps on jabbing*
*like an edged piece of gravel.*
*This wounded heart.*
*The unknown tumultuous dance*
*at the shrine-*
*the shiny green shrine.*
*From the mosque emerge*
*a few breaths, redolent of patience.*
*Salves to heal*
*the wounds of a naked child.*
*The mother looks on, full of hope.*
*The caps are yellow,*
*maybe pale in colour.*
*This pallor,*
*this pallor which uses*
*its fingertips to keep a count.*
*That's the first day*
*of a new century.*

# THE NIGHT DESCENDS INTO THE LAKE

*The night descends into*
*the still waters of the lake.*
*Moonlight adrift in the woods.*
*Wild flowers of silken hues*
*hide themselves in the nearby grass.*
*Dust inflamed*
*by the torrid moments.*

*Thoughts entangled within words.*
*An utterance the lips*
*can only muddle through,*
*exactly like the night descending*
*into the still waters of the lake,*
*like moonlight adrift in the woods.*

## THE NIGHT OF ASCENSION

*Apparently, another ordinary night,*
*Just like any other night,*
*but how can anyone imagine*
*that in the course of this night*
*of the month of Rajab*
*a Traveller has already set forth*
*from a house in Hateem*
*for the Al-Aqsa mosque*
*and from there will rise to heaven.*
*A straight line of light ascending*
*from the earth to the sky.*
*Why call it a line? It's a holy trail.*

*What can I say to glorify*
*the Traveller, someone so honourable*
*his journey without a precedent*
*and the speed at which he travels*
*is a miracle in itself.*

# THE SMOKE

*The familiar fog*
*of an impenetrable winter,*
*as the evening putting on*
*the mask of black night*
*drifted through your street*

*Far off,*
*near the forlorn windows*
*of the furthest house*
*a thought, a bit like a light,*
*flickered and went out.*
*Even now there about*
*a question, like smoke,*
*drifts from place to place!*

## *THE SEASON OF KITE-FLYING WAS OVER*

*The season of spring, of kite-flying*
*was over. No one knew*
*who held in his hand*
*the other end*
*of the string.*
*There was not a bird in sight*
*near or far,*
*not even a kite.*
*Even the green earth below*
*had nothing but gashes to show.*
*Only the sky was lit up by the sun.*
*The shabby houses in Mozang,*
*rendered speechless,*
*sprouting from the cadaverous*
*and run-down*
*threshold of the century;*
*and on the roofs of these houses*
*or what remains*
*of the roofs, something akin*
*to a forest attains*

*a germination and within*
*the layers of a snuffed-out noise*
*a stillness smoulders.*
*The season of spring, of kite-flying*
*was over.*

## *THE SNOWMAN*

*My snowman,*
*this dazzling, glittering life of yours,*
*how long is it going to last?*
*Till it rains?*
*Till the sun begins to shine?*
*That's it.*

*What a pity!*
*Water and warmth,*
*which mean life to me,*
*spell your doom.*

*Tell me*
*why were you made?*
*Only as a plaything?*
*Do you know why?*
*I wonder*
*What I was created for?*
*Just to live,*
*to bring the fleeting sequence*
*of breathing in and out*
*to a conclusion?*

*You melt away*
*as the rain comes down.*
*You melt away*
*in the sun's bright glare.*
*I am melting down*
*in the blinding heat*
*of my thoughts;*
*I am all on fire*
*in the smouldering body*
*of a quest.*
*I wonder,*
*why were you made,*
*why was I created?*

*From One Loneliness to Another*

# *Reflections*

*From One Loneliness to Another*

## *1947*

*With the shades of the past*
*tied up in bundles*
*a doddering migration*
*is on the move, alongside*
*those millions of moments*
*which will traverse*
*the dream like distance*
*spread over hundreds of years.*
*Is the land historic or it's grief?*
*Who would give it a thought*
*how can the sleeping particles of sand*
*which belong to the struggling night*
*change the day's orientation?*
*Pale voices pierced right through*
*as they move*
*from one acacia tree to another.*
*A few colourless birds cling to the branches.*
*The morning's reddish tone, slightly blackish.*
*The vanished waves of the River Ravi.*
*The dull winds of the unknown season*
*reiterate the emptiness.*

*From One Loneliness to Another*

*Indifferent smoke rising from the heart's tent,*
*a wet chain*
*of senseless esteem.*
*A severance?*
*A separation?*
*or a bleached horizon?*
*Freedom walks coquettishly down a road flooded*
*with tender sunlight*
*and kicks up dust.*
*A blood-red turban of honour*
*slipping from the head,*
*beyond memories.*

# A LONG DISTANCE CALL

*Listen to me, my love,*
*before the burden*
*of seeking the acquaintance*
*of what's not known,*
*accompanied by winds*
*which crumble at their edges,*
*goes down to the ford*
*where memories coloured*
*by twilight hues*
*speak of devastated nights,*
*where the sand, the smothered sand,*
*recounts the laments*
*of the river Ravi*
*which exists no more.*

*A somewhat crazy strain,*
*a vagrant tune,*
*hear it, my love, again.*

*Come, let us lay to rest somewhere*

*our griefs which are falling apart*
*in these silent forests*
*where nothing seems to stir,*
*within the dismal wrinkles of a fir.*

## *COMPULSION*

*And way beyond the deep blue wilderness*
*the magic of things growing up.*
*The dreary doors of a slightly dusky sleep*
*opening as the wind knocks on them.*
*In the empty space the pain in tatters.*
*And the thin leaves of a dream*
*begging to shield themselves*
*against a blunt sound.*
*Barbed words on the shores of silence.*
*The crowded verse of despair*
*captioning the facelessness of stars*
*made itself manifest.*
*Thin strips of shrinking, restive clouds*
*like winged migrations*
*outrunning the homing in birds.*
*A fragile glassy flight*
*in the line of fire*
*of a journey's pallid shrapnel.*
*Did the sky display*
*a reflection or sheer smog?*
*The ashen stripes of a snuffed-out rainbow*

across the appearance of a bewildered rose
drenched in the heavy August showers.
The tear drop of a woe, lilac hued,
awakens in the sad pupils of the eyes.
The earth desired to set itself free
from what the word existence meant.
Its protest made sense.
The compulsion to germinate
is after all a compulsion.

## I WONDER WHY

*A shower of small change.*
*Coins fall as the ashen cloud*
*unties its knot;*
*and many memories tinkle down*
*on the reddish floor*
*of shining bricks.*
*The transparent drops of clean rainwater*
*drum out a beat*
*on the hot tin roof,*
*off-colour tunes swirling about*
*in the rain-washed courtyard.*
*Steam rises from a cooking clay pot*
*Smoke rises from the clay hearth*
*stinging the eyes of the birds*
*huddling up in the old guava tree.*
*A dream appears*
*like a bamboo broom*
*A lane reverberating*
*with longings comes to life again.*
*Ramshackle and lime-washed yellow tenements*

*and those who live in them crumbly like sand.*
*I wonder why*
*each time I open my eyes*
*I see the same watery scene*
*again and again?*

## *MONTAGE*

*What passion drives the waves*
*of the pallid sea, lines after lines?*
*The moon, the prismatic moon,*
*shaped like a lovely fish,*
*fastens poems on watery arches.*
*... the poem will begin something like this.*

*I have them ensnared*
*even now, the words and colours.*
*How many distances still lie*
*in the coming months and years?*
*The memories of a vanished spring,*
*like snails covered with moss,*
*turn brittle, resembling the pages*
*of tattered manuscripts.*
*The seasons, festooning the doors,*
*speak of wounds.*

*Look at the loneliness,*
*scattered around like seashells,*
*from the balcony of your house*
*in Cologne*

*From One Loneliness to Another*

*or from the shore of the poem.*

*Look!*

*In what manner the heart's island*

*gets buried under a dream unseen.*

*Another spell of hours,*

*made up of words, comes to an end.*

*Somewhere underneath the time another time is on the move.*

*…The poem will pause here for a while to catch her breath.*

*The whiteness and the blue*

*filtering through*

*the seashells and the cathedrals;*

*the foaming waves, the waters,*

*a valley, a breeze and a few words*

*of prayers, words*

*which taste like salt.*

*Let us see towards which landfall*

*the waves of words and colours*

*are headed. What passion drives*

*the waves of the pallid sea,*

*lines drawn on lines?*

*From One Loneliness to Another*

*What do the soft sounds*
*of the flickering moments say?*
*Who knows from what alien lands away*
*would the sands drift this way*
*to make sense of it all*

*... The poem will reach this point and come to an end.*

## ON A BED MADE OF STRINGS

*The moon lit the way*
*to lead my eyes into sadness.*

*The silence transmuted away*
*into poetry and before long*
*it became a story*
*and thereafter slowly*
*changed into a song.*

*The threadbare sheet*
*on the bed made of strings*
*seemed like a soft, enticing*
*bedding to an errant dream.*
*Many a time, as I*
*covered myself up*
*in a sleep carded and combed.*
*I could recall the gentle*
*caresses of the night.*
*I could remember*
*until the sunrise*
*all the light-hued butterflies.*

*As the day unfolded,*
*the colours, one by one,*
*faded away and none*
*of the wounds had any*
*more sting left. The memory*
*in a blaze*
*had still a part to play.*
*The moon lit the way*
*to lead my eyes into sadness.*

## *ON THE DAMP WALL OF THOSE DAYS*

*Those were the days when dreams*
*grew in the windows.*
*The vision ricocheted*
*off the flower vase.*

*The scenes sorted out*
*what a colour meant to them.*
*During the icy night*
*congealed over the hill*
*the birds weaved dreams*
*until the new sun's rising.*

*And the playful, ticklish*
*and silken flurry of wind*
*beside the green branches.*

*Do you remember anything?*
*When the evening chasing*
*a firefly lost its way*
*in the flame-like raspberry bushes.*

*A rustling fear checked*
*the woodland's incursion.*

*From One Loneliness to Another*

*On the damp wall of those days*
*vines reeled about in the wind.*

*But we couldn't touch them*
*even though we stood up on our toes.*

*We don't know if the green-coloured,*
*moss-covered wall was too high*
*or our hands too small.*

*If, by chance, we were*
*to come to that place again*
*we may well discover*
*what does the interplay*
*of those scenes and seasons*
*and the days steeped in dreams*
*turn out to be or mean?*

*How do the diverging confines*
*of childhood and youth*
*merge with each other?*

*If we were to visit*
*the place again*
*we may find out.*

*From One Loneliness to Another*

## *REMORSE*

*From the unfurling*

*of a being*

*as a word to the environs*

*of a wound*

*inflicted by a dream,*

*blessed visions in untidy garbs*

*blossom athwart and about*

*a journey branching out.*

*Sapless berries of the twilight's rosy hues*

*in the white*

*thickets or maybe the fireflies*

*have shed their raiments of light to bury them in the spherical*

*convolutions which belong*

*to the hoary sky.*

*Slate-grey clouds throng*

*the outskirts of the soul,*

*right from the pinnacle*

*of the snowfields*

*to the chasm of the moon.*

*The burnt-out testament*

*as the evening of the absent*
*dead makes the sun disappear.*
*Hemmed in by a surge*
*of colours right up to despair*
*of a reply which doesn't dare*
*to be without prevarication,*
*a question still remains*
*behind the haze*
*of the mirror.*
*Only the reflection persists*
*of the remorse of convalescent days*

## *SHOULD YOU COME ACROSS HER, TELL HER*

*Listen, you!*
*Tipsy wind*
*of a lovely evening,*
*should you come across her, tell her*
*that these songs*
*of colourful warblers,*
*the rainbow in the rainy days*
*which steals its colours*
*from flowers,*
*the perfumed paths*
*suffused with partial sunlight,*
*and the trees lost in thought,*
*as they lean over the roadways,*
*and the branches in a trance*
*entangled with each other,*
*and the shiny and sweet-smelling*
*greenery beyond the lake*
*and scenes shrouded*
*in a blue haze*
*through which the rain comes down*

*From One Loneliness to Another*

*in a gentle rhythm,*
*the waking up, asleep*
*and inebriated seasons,*
*all these don't stir*
*her memories in my heart,*
*nor do they make*
*a sweet fire blaze up again*
*which has been dormant.*

*You!*
*Tipsy wind*
*of a lovely evening,*
*should you come across her tell her*
*nothing at all.*

## *THE JOURNEY WOULD BEGIN*

*Our dreams float*
*on the gentle current*
*of the wind.*
*If you can but do it,*
*turn your eyes*
*into whirlpools.*

*It is very likely*
*that the desires*
*now in a state of flux*
*can again be snared.*

*Just give it a thought!*

*What difference is there,*
*after all, in remaining*
*cooped up in a cage*
*or in getting out*
*from a trap of shining tears?*
*It takes only a single breath:*
*either you stay put on this side*
*or cross over to the other shore.*

*From One Loneliness to Another*

*But do all the dreamboats*
*manage to reach a landfall*
*where it may be possible*
*to interpret what they mean?*
*The whirlpools of the eyes*
*are there to waylay them.*
*Set off on your journey.*
*Who can say where*
*the butterflies would by and by*
*be able to fly*
*and the sails*
*of the reluctant leaves unfurl.*

*From One Loneliness to Another*

## THE LAST LEAF FROM THE DIARY OF A
## MISSING COLUMBUS

*I have to cross a sea of blind questions,*
*holding on to the wind's hand.*
*The vessel of words and meanings*
*seeks out seashores.*

*Possibility is a blue star, facing the wind.*
*The rising wave is also a metaphor*
*shifting its burden*
*from one shoulder to the other.*

*With help of this metaphor*
*I have to cross*
*a sea of unending questions.*
*I can't find a seashore.*

*A moment ago, a desolate wave*
*of thought came this way.*
*It asked me:*
*"Son of Yazdani,*
*Is this a boat...?*
*Or a straw...?"*
*The wrecked vessel of words and meanings*

*From One Loneliness to Another*

*trapped in the whirlpool*
*of concentric blind questions*
*is in a spin,*
*creaking and gasping for breath.*

*The sails look like threads*
*from a winding sheet,*
*And the waves---they keep on shifting*
*their burden from one shoulder*
*to the other.*

*The desolation of water,*
*beating its breast, stands*
*impeding my way.*

*I have to cross a sea*
*of blind questions.*

*I can't find exit*
*from this rampart of water.*
*I can't find a way*
*to wriggle out of my questions.*
*I can't find a seashore.*
*I simply can't.*

## *TRANSIT*

*A dream falls apart again.*
*It would take a while*
*before a new dream begins*

## *THE NIGHT*

*They say:*
*Night has already fallen.*
*But no dreams home in*
*on the expectant*
*skyline of the eyes.*
*Face to face with*
*such lonesome,*
*cold and lifeless*
*and somewhat unfamiliar*
*darkness fused together with darkness,*
*how can anyone know*
*with any certitude that he exists.*

## *THE SONG*

*The leaves fall*
*in a slow cadence.*
*The smouldering colors*
*give off smoke.*
*A song of autumn*
*is on fire somewhere.*
*A bonfire of all*
*the musical notes*
*lights up the horizon.*
*A song of autumn*
*unwinds somewhere.*

# *Places*

*From One Loneliness to Another*

## *ALL THESE ALLEYS BELONG TO ME*

*Daubed with a sullen light,*
*crouching down*
*in an inveterate mist,*
*sweltering beside the river Ravi,*
*setting in motion clouds of dust*
*which roll past like waves,*
*asleep as well as awake,*
*all these alleys belong to me,*
*intimately mine.*
*And there is one*
*which seems to be*
*the most misshapen and rickety*
*of them all,*
*like a spidery scrawl,*
*where in soft evening's shadow*
*lie in complete disarray*
*the memories of my golden years.*

## *A LONELY WEEKEND*

*In the Central Park*

*a somewhat errant moon*

*belonging, who can say,*

*to which bygone age.*

*The mist whispers*

*as it cascades down*

*the Empire State Building,*

*conceals itself*

*from streets which gape at it*

*and opens its eyes in Brooklyn.*

*The chimneys spew darkness or perhaps clouds!*

*The pale light of the cemetery*

*makes a mockery*

*of the Statue of Liberty.*

*The lookalike sadness*

*of senile days*

*looks down from the balcony.*

*On the Fifty-third street*

*rubber plants*

*behind a leather sofa,*

*a cherry wood table,*

*made in Italy, in the front*
*Insignificant news featuring*
*Whites on a 56-inch LCD*
*Far away from the front page*
*of the "Times",*
*completely indifferent*
*to the Wall Street shenanigans,*
*there sits on a deserted sidewalk*
*a lonely weekend.*

# A POEM FOR LAHORE

*You were lost in deep sleep*
*when I left you.*
*I went away without saving goodbye.*
*What else could I have done…?*
*I had to go.*
*In the morning, as you rubbed your eyes,*
*you may have seen,*
*where your silken shadow fell,*
*in the leaves streaming past,*
*a leaf…!*
*A dry, wan and distraught leaf,*
*like my departing kiss.*

## *COLOGNE*

*I first came across the evening*
*in a forest*
*where the unfrequented path*
*lay in the shadows.*

*The moon disappeared*
*in the fog.*
*The clouds descended*
*on the still waters of a lake.*
*The wind gone astray*
*in a region without bearings,*
*told ancient tales.*

*Where my loneliness*
*came to a turning,*
*which was wet all over,*
*there I found silence---*
*a silence falling leaf by leaf,*
*becoming frightened*
*of sleep's sapless branches,*
*falling asleep beside*
*the shadow cast by a branch,*

*From One Loneliness to Another*

*even transfixing its fear*
*with a succession of sobs.*

*I first came across the evening*
*in a forest*
*where the unfrequented path*
*lay in the shadows.*

## *DAY, LIGHT OR SAVING*

*A night in November,*

*waning and waxing,*

*passes sluggishly away.*

*Once again there is*

*nothing to share*

*with anyone*

*in the crowd's spillover,*

*chock-a-block.*

*I alone belong to it.*

*A thickish*

*buzz on the road.*

*A light adrift*

*and beyond*

*the half-open windows*

*a denuded field,*

*well-trimmed grass,*

*a damp silence*

*or a transparent dark.*

*Even the freshness*

*perhaps is vanishing.*

*But how can it be helped?*

*A blue list*
*on the door of the fridge:*
*bills to be paid,*
*send the scanner for repair,*
*reschedule appointment with the new physician,*
*have to post*
*the latest poem on Facebook,*
*have to turn the clocks*
*back by an hour,*
*have to make a phone call.*
*Lahore?*
*Cologne??*
*Dhaka???*

## FENCED IN BY LANDSCAPES

*Moon in the clouds as they rustle along.*
*A few fireflies in the russet bushes.*
*The imperceptible heartbeat of the night*
*becomes slow, even slower.*

*A blue reflection in a green mirror.*
*A sky lowering a little*
*on the still lake.*

*A plain, untarnished paint-brush.*
*Flamboyant birds*
*on the shores which spin out dreams.*
*It seems time is passing*
*even more slowly than before.*

*Only the wind weaves*
*the leaning trees*
*and from every*
*plant branch retrieves*
*one colour only.*
*As the sun melts down*
*on the other side*
*of the red twilight*

*From One Loneliness to Another*

*a sorrow emerges*
*from the aperture*
*of an evening on fire.*

*My fireflies,*
*My heartbeat,*
*My branches,*
*My sun.*

*Who has portioned me out*
*into so many scenes?*

*Not a single wall*
*of the exhibition hall*
*is bare.*

# FROM THE SHORE OF A DREAM

*My Cologne! Life of my life!*
*Life of my life! We shall meet again!*
*Either on the threshold of time*
*or on the other side of desires.*

*But don't worry*
*I will write you letters*
*from the shore of every dream;*
*from the vicinity of those forests*
*which sway as they dance*
*to a capricious tune of waves;*
*whose silence goes warbling about*
*through your heartbeat and mine.*

*The vines on a slope*
*by the banks of a river.*
*The soft blue approach of the sky*
*in the gleaming waters.*

*Stars, glittering hours.*
*The evening blending with Rhine.*

*I have gathered the season*
*of memory drop by drop.*
*But someone, between breaths,*
*says that we shall meet again.*
*We shall bloom again*
*amid fragrant, glimmering scene.*

*As yet the sails stand still*
*but in a little while*
*the anchor of migration would be lifted.*

## GOOD NIGHT NEW YORK

*The session of small brown birds*
*is over. So, who is it*
*the barbecue's ashes speak to?*
*The show goes on*
*from Jackson Heights to Coney Island.*
*The red stars, almost wringing wet,*
*come and cling to the coloured*
*windowpanes of a bar.*
*Swinging lights across a bridge*
*which is lost in a reverie.*
*The traffic signals turn on and off*
*by fits and starts.*
*Eyelashes droop as if weighed down.*
*A pointless frenzy of wheels*
*from Manhattan to JFK,*
*as some orange-coloured misgivings,*
*some murky wounds,*
*fill the void left behind*
*by cars which go by and speed away.*
*For heaven's sake, make*

*From One Loneliness to Another*

*this ungainly rhapsody of restiveness*
*come to a stop.*
*The New York night*
*now wants to fall asleep.*

## *IN A CYBER CAFÉ*

*The feverish finger-joints*
*wish to hear*
*the scene's loneliness,*
*while from the mirror of void*
*it seems as if autumn*
*is glaring at you.*
*A search through digits*
*after digits made up of a misplaced*
*number of memories.*
*Someone's voice which throws open*
*the door of dreams*
*begins to go up in flames*
*in the soul's emptiness.*
*Far away,*
*at the bottom of the sea it seems*
*as if the ring tone of a phone*
*has reached a boiling point.*
*Windows begin to light up*
*on a screen which had been*
*blank for a very long time.*

*From One Loneliness to Another*

## *IN CENTRAL PARK*

*An almost weary light*
*cast by the dismal lamppost.*
*A smell smothered*
*by a tree.*
*Who has stolen*
*the moon away?*
*No idea at all*
*how many times again*
*should one now*
*rummage in the night's wallet,*
*open one's email*
*on the blackberry*
*sprouting in the palm.*

## MANHATTAN

*Hemmed in by skyscrapers*
*a somewhat unfamiliar familiarity gazes downwards*
*at the clouds.*
*From the window of half-open eyes*
*a moment comes to stop*
*at the Time Square, holding*
*a sign which lights up, goes out.*
*Is it life or a yellow cab*
*which blows its horn and passes by?*
*A police car, an ambulance,*
*a noise fading out suddenly,*
*paving the way to death.*
*Countless feet slowly*
*move towards Broadway*
*"Proceed to the nearest road",*
*the navigator cries out.*
*Blue Tooth germinates in the ear.*
*How long can anyone*
*remain on one's feet, in panic*
*within the evening of a cold forest?*

*From One Loneliness to Another*

*A glance, begging for a response,*
*turns the corner.*
*How empty is this crowded city*
*like the inbox of my dreams.*

## *MID-DAY*

*A window*
*opening on autumn*
*A window.*
*The shiny floor*
*of the kitchen.*
*The slack, staggering*
*sunlight fades away.*
 *An ordinary day.*
*A light, dusty,*
*dull brown breeze*
*picks up.*
*A sandy hopefulness*
*on the point of vanishing*
*in the eyes*
*the tree holds the key*
*to that courtyard*
*beside which lies*
*the stilled river*
*of your memory.*
*An ordinary day.*
*A window.*

*From One Loneliness to Another*

*A breeze.*
*A light, dusty,*
*dull brown breeze.*
*Mid-day…*

## *NIAGARA FALLS*

*A rush of faces streaming past.*
*Swirling and rolling waves,*
*a semblance of tourists on the move*
*as they make their way towards*
*the window of the unknown.*

*On their shoulders the rusty stain*
*of seen and unseen worlds.*

*Distorted maps of a pallid wind.*
*A tree-lined way gone missing.*
*The sunlight of bewilderment*
*on the eyelashes.*

*Rainbow colours in shreds.*
*Blue jeans, golden complexions.*
*A cold reminder of December*
*in mid-April.*

*Numb with fear the sun*
*goes and crouches in a corner*

*of a wilting evening,*

*just like a child*

*who tries to avoid the steady gaze*

*of alien eyes.*

## *ONLY FOR A MOMENT OR SO*

*No, we won't tarry here much longer,*
*only for a moment or so.*
*We have nothing at all to do*
*with these badly lit narrow streets,*
*these ramshackle houses,*
*these forlorn shops.*

*We have to unburden*
*ourselves of an obligation,*
*to pay back what we owe*
*to memories long forgotten*
*City of Lahore!*
*We have to give back only a story,*
*memento of a journey,*
*a youth, known incompletely.*
*Maybe.*

*From One Loneliness to Another*

## ON RIVER RHINE'S BANK

*These silken, humming*
*and capricious waves of Rhine,*
*which weave dreams*
*of lovely memories, of rainy days*
*flooding the land*
*in their wake.*

*The waves sift out*
*the dissolving reflections*
*of the beautiful evening's glittering scenes,*
*and these wayward, gentle*
*blue breezes of the scented city*
*also carry with them*
*the velvet like sense*
*of someone's touch.*

*The unfamiliar gusts*
*which assail my furrowed*
*brow wish to share my secrets.*
*The concentric waves roll in*
*and brush my feet.*
*They assume the form*

*of rusty chains of a broken promise,*
*cling to my feet,*
*yearning for a promise*
*which would hold good*
*in the days to come.*

*But, I, an unfaithful being,*
*mercurial, a rolling stone,*
*who trades in words,*
*what commitment can I make*
*to these waves*
*I am not even familiar with?*

## *PAINTING AN OBSOLETE SEASON*

*These damp walls and doors*
*of my room;*
*and the yellow, jaundiced*
*creepers which cling to them.*

*A sobbing silence in the roots.*

*A nameless soft sound*
*caressing the brown branches.*
*A strange rustling.*
*Is it a journey which begins*
*in a dream and ends*
*by turning into dust…?*

*An obsolete season.*

*Snuffed out heartbeats.*
*Desires which disperse*
*like shadows falling on shadows.*
*Desires, heartbeats, windows.*

*A wardrobe.*

*A somewhat rough-hewn*
*and mouldering wardrobe*
*and a painting placed on top of it.*
*A gilded frame*
*and leaves, covered with dust,*
*shooting up from it.*

*Wind…*
*In faded colours*
*and in a silence which becomes*
*more and more intense,*
*the pages of a diary*
*blow in the wind.*

*Autumn, silence, heartbeats,*
*heartbeats, windows, silence.*
*Silence.*
*Silence.*
*…Life.*

## THE FINAL EVENING OF A BYGONE CENTURY

*A sleepy weariness preceding sleep.*
*A lantern, like pallor in the chest*
*sobs on and on in the heartbeats*
*resembling a paralyzed light.*
*A noise of looms or of breathing,*
*the warp and woof all jumbled up.*
*The train doesn't stop anywhere.*
*Look, all the seats are unoccupied.*
*You can sit down wherever you like.*
*Time has come to a halt and life*
*seems to be in a hurry.*
*Dead insect, a plastic sandal,*
*heedlessness, a belch and retching.*
*Who would now bother*
*to clean up the floor?*
*Words that quiver like whistles.*
*A few toothless homilies,*
*like the pain one feels*
*when the last tooth falls out.*
*How close gathers the night,*

*From One Loneliness to Another*

*how far away the destinations drift.*
*Dishes lie in heaps on the table.*
*Pain, Alzheimer, diabetes,*
*tablets, all mixed up*
*in a haphazard memory.*
*The meal is ready. Let's eat it now.*
*Yes, but shut the windows lest*
*the distances still to be traversed*
*barge in again.*

*From One Loneliness to Another*

# *Dreams*

# *FROM ONE LONELINESS TO ANOTHER*

*The sweet smell of buds*
*entranced as they remember someone---*
*no idea, who they remember;*
*the reflections of damp*
*moments in the lake,*
*the sparkling playfulness*
*of candid sunlight,*
*the light breeze as a faint,*
*pale evening draws near,*
*the ashen silence*
*of greenery fading into yellow,*
*the soft patter of raindrops*
*as they strike half-open flowers*
*and an open umbrella,*
*while the rain comes down*
*with a sibilant sound,*
*the moonlight feeling shy*
*in the night's presence*
*and withdrawing into itself,*
*the phosphorescence of fireflies*
*managing to escape*

*From One Loneliness to Another*

*from a closed fist,*

*you---and the soft approach*

*of your dream---*

*all these accompany me*

*as I migrate*

*from one loneliness to another.*

# DURING THE TIRED RAINS OF SEPTEMBER

*In the jungle of black gravestones,*
*the bewildered birds of prayers*
*flop their wings.*
*The night crouches*
*in the rustling bushes of wind.*

*Are these dreams that wail*
*or yellow earth piled up*
*to mark the graves?*

*The flowers of smoke*
*fall apart, like petals.*

*Who bothers to listen*
*to the dreary legends*
*of wet and crumbled leaves*
*during the tired rains*
*of September?*

*New hymns arise*
*from old caravans.*
*The burnt-out blue incense stick*

*sleeps as if a part of the escort of silence.*

*It seems that life itself,*
*its head resting on the shoulder*
*of death in convulsions,*
*is weeping endlessly.*

## *GHAZAL*

*A moment passing endlessly till eternity.*
*The snow kept falling.*
*Life's earthen cup repeatedly filled or empty.*
*The snow kept falling.*

*A century falling asleep, oblivious,*
*like the news of a day gone by. The new era,*
*torn to shreds, diffusing constantly.*
*The snow kept falling.*

*Who went down, stair by stair, stealthily*
*through a phase of memory,*
*down into the dream's underground room?*
*The snow kept falling.*

*Time passing by in the shadow of the lake,*
*and again and again the melting heart.*
*A stillness making its way through the mirror.*
*The snow kept falling.*

*Two pale purple blossoms blazed on and on*
*upon a dazzling white sheet. The moon*

*shivered all the time, deep in its journey.*
*The snow kept falling.*

*In endless reflections, the desire never losing*
*its vividness nor the season its fragrance.*
*In mirrors without end, she kept on adding to her*
*charms.*
*The snow kept falling.*

*One canvas only and just a single colour*
*as far as the eyes could see.*
*A moment passing endlessly till eternity.*
*The snow kept falling.*

## *IF YOU WERE HERE*

*If you were here,*
*we would pick the flowers*
*of these fragrant hours*
*and find a way*
*by cutting right across*
*the evening's tipsy breeze,*
*weave a scene out of the dreams*
*which lie scattered in our eyes,*
*walk in the shade of drowsy trees,*
*make our memories blossom forth*
*from the soggy pathways,*
*steep our breath in the nice smell*
*rising from the dark grey earth,*
*feel the touch of mellow moonlight,*
*spread out the chilly sunshine*
*in our house's courtyard,*
*adorn our lips with honeyed silence,*
*wipe out the gloom from our hearts*
*with the hum of a song*
*heard softly beside us;*
*forget everything.*
*Only if you were here.*

*From One Loneliness to Another*

# IN A CRACKLING NIGHT

*Although the night is lonely*
*I don't feel lonely.*
*Although the moon is lonely*
*I don't feel lonely.*

*The moonlight bathed in fragrance*
*rising from the wild flowers.*
*The reflections of half-awake*
*and half-asleep trees*
*in these dimly lit waters.*

*Something like whispers*
*heavy with dew,*
*on an icy bench*
*in a wintry season.*

*Small hours of the night.*
*The lines of an unwritten poem*
*which follow the jumbled up*
*tune of memories.*

*As I walk on the cold grass*

*of drizzly moments*
*I can feel the sound*
*of your steps in my breath.*

*No, I don't feel lonely.*
*It is the crackling night*
*which is lonely.*

*No, I don't feel lonely.*
*It is the moon,*
*which has lost its way,*
*which is lonely.*

## *JUST BEFORE REACHING A DECISION*

*My dear!*
*Wash off the cold memories*
*of the night that's gone*
*and fill your shawl*
*with the new day's*
*sweet smelling sunshine.*

*Listen, my dear!*
*Today is alive.*
*Yesterday is gone.*
*To live is to breathe*
*in and out in a rhythm.*
*It is not an inert instant.*

*If you try to while*
*this lovely evening away*
*by indulging in jumbled up talk*
*peculiar to these times*
*your life will be buried under*
*the dust raised*
*by these insipid moments.*

*From One Loneliness to Another*

Tomorrow the astray wind
of these very hours
would be lost in the pale
courtyard of this age
or, at times, would weave a song
and hurl itself
into the despoiled poplars.
Yes, the cloud of resentment
would spread apart
but the evening would go by.

Therefore, my dear,
wash off the cold memories
of the night that's gone
and fill your shawl
with the new day's
sweet smelling sunshine;
because life is here and now,
life is not a Yesterday.
a day;
already gone by.

## *O CHEERFUL, ELEGENT LADY*

*O cheerful, elegant lady,*
*I know quite well*
*that the dark shade of my being,*
*with which you are not familiar,*
*are of no account*
*in your domain of sun*
*and brilliant light.*

*The grass here torn up*
*by the feet of young men*
*over fond of jogging.*

*The wind clings*
*to the wet mass of the seashore.*
*A glimmering pathway*
*in the wasteland of breathing.*

*A sound which beats*
*its head against time.*
*Perhaps this sound is my life!*

*My dream is a useless coin*

*From One Loneliness to Another*

*of East Germany*
*which has no value at all*
*in a reunified Germany.*
*And my vision stands deprived*
*of even the silvery clink*
*of a dream coming true.*

*My longings have been lost perhaps,*
*just as if far away*
*from a welcoming gaze,*
*an old, musty painting*
*moves along on a river,*
*like the steamboats belonging*
*to a century which has ended.*

*What I search for,*
*in the colours of the tulips*
 *which flourish in your window,*
*in the incompletely watched TV shows*
*and in the tangled up*
*light purple trailing plant,*
*is nowhere to be found.*
*O cheerful, elegant lady,*
*I don't even look your way!*

*From One Loneliness to Another*

## *POETS*

*All that we know*
*is how to set the words on fire.*
*We do not know*
*that the burning words*
*warm up those feelings*
*which are chilled to the bone!*

*They impart*
*a little bit heat*
*to frozen thought*
*and lifeless reality.*
*They provide a hint of warmth*
*to shivering dreams*
*and tired out breath.*

*We do not know*
*what the burning words imply.*
*All that we know*
*is how to set the words on fire.*

## SOMEWHERE IN TIME'S FOREST

Somewhere in the depths
of a densely wooded place
in the dark, silent nooks
and crannies of the heart,
in the fragrant instants
of these days,
there, in the declining shades
of trees in leaf,
in these branches
bending down in sadness,
on these warbling ways
where the waters are a dazzle
mirroring the playful sunlight,
in the swirling wind
of these endless days,
following a forlorn,
zigzagging path,
I am letting, my love,
your memory fade away.

## *WHEN THE WIND WOULD BLOW*

*When the wind would blow*
*again next year*
*with the rainy season's advent*
*and a ray would smile*
*from within*
*the cluster of wet leaves*
*high up on a tree,*
*perhaps you won't*
*even remember me.*

## *BUTTERFLIES*

*How bright is the night!*
*Although my beloved's gone.*
*Blossoms of the rays*
*of a grief unfold among the sad*
*vines of moonlight.*
*Past moments turn*
*into butterflies*
*and disappear.*
*No matter how hard*
*you look for them*
*in the cozy resting places*
*of the night*
*you won't come across*
*them ever again.*

## *THE VALLEY*

*Poetry displeased with words*
*and dreams distance*
*themselves from the eyes.*
*Moonlight shies away*
*from the moon.*
*But you alone*
*are a resplendent sight*
*far away from the dampness*
*of a leafy recess.*
*It is a mystery why*
*I think of you now*
*in a valley where*
*profound silence reigns,*
*with my heart bereft*
*of sorrow or desire.*

## *A LAMENT*

*Words like*
*impounded shores*
*dissolve and vanish*
*in the terse nightfall.*
*Time is a derelict boat.*
*The wind reels about as gusts*
*chase gusts.*
*Whose wings are these*
*widespread and beating*
*in the air?*
*Whose accent the wind*
*takes on to speak*
*from days no longer*
*familiar to us?*
*Our griefs lie all around us*
*like smashed up horoscopes.*
*The memory*
*anchored to decay.*
*The poem ensnared in the sails.*

# *Relations*

*From One Loneliness to Another*

## *A DREAM ON THE WINGS OF BUTTERFLIES*

*How stale is sleep?*

*How fresh the dream?*

*What a new dream indeed!*

*A dream whose body's golden gleam*

*is hard to interpret or read*

*in the light of my past*

*which is but a dream*

*within a dream*

*or so it seems.*

*The dream issues*

*from the matrix of the eyes*

*and comes to rest as it lies*

*on the lap of dawn.*

*Through how many dark passages*

*does the dream proceed?*

*A newly blossoming dream,*

*a dream utterly fresh indeed,*

*comes to rest on my palm*

*like a drop of dew.*

*Its shining brow lit*

*From One Loneliness to Another*

*up with such a brilliant hue*

*that destiny itself*

*could not stand it.*

*A rainbow nestles in its shadow.*

*A soft breeze hums*

*as it tries to keep up with it as it turns*

*from one side to the other*

*in its sleep.*

*Each time it breathes*

*perfumed rays emanate from it*

*drenched with rainy clouds.*

*But the flower-like fists remain closed. It seems*

*as if there is another dream,*

*a heavenly, fragrant dream,*

*within the fists, a tiny and somewhat delicate dream.*

*Mindful of all this*

*I cannot convince myself to open his fist,*

*afraid that the dream inscribed*

*on the wings of butterflies,*

*the dream sifting through*

*the lovely shades of desires might take flight*

*From One Loneliness to Another*

*and fade away.*
*I keep thinking of the possibilities,*
*afraid that its tiny palm, like my eyes,*
*would remain open with surprise,*
*waiting to the end of our days,*
*for something to happen,*
*for someone to arrive,*
*may keep a forlorn lookout,*
*like butterflies which belong*
*to a dream and slip away from a tender fist*
*and go on wandering about*
*amidst leaves of grass throughout life's long*
*and troubled course.*
*Mindful that all this may come to pass*
*I don't open his fist,*
*I don't throw open*
*the windows of my house.*

*(For Zernaab)*

## *A SELFIE*

*Who are you, stranger…?*

*What dream have you come from? Speak…?*
*How come you look so much like me!*
*I have seen you somewhere before but where?*

*Perhaps far away from my vision.*
*Perhaps through the looking glass*
*or beyond disconnected words*
*lost beside an agreeable dream---*
*with a sadness smouldering in you*
*because you couldn't interpret the dream,*
*or on the bank of blue Rhine,*
*in a drunken state which became a part*
*of a church's shadow…!*
*or on the bright sea of golden sunlight*
*clinging to a threadbare and lifeless sail;*
*or during the course of a night*
*vanishing within the haze of clouds;*
*or dozing in the light*
*of these bulbs on the verge of flickering out;*

*From One Loneliness to Another*

or while gleaning on the seashores

the signs of an evening's soft approach;

wrapped in the dust of moonlight

on a road which comes from far away;

far from the inebriated hours

near the stilled distances;

getting wet in the rain that falls on damp and yellow
leaves;

or among the crumbling bricks of the deserted ruins
of time;

or getting in a tiff with oneself on a moss-covered
bench

in a garden adjacent

to an empty corridor of Alhambra;

or in the fiery winds

which blow across Sarajevo.


Perhaps I have seen you in these landscapes;

or in ashes carried by the wind in these blazing
scenes.


But exactly where…?

Perhaps far away from my vision

Perhaps through the looking glass.

*From One Loneliness to Another*

*Speak…!*

*Who are you, stranger?*

*What dream have you come from?*

*Speak…!*

## *A SILENCE REMAINS TO BE UTTERED*

*I live a silence,*
*with a shining nothingness*
*close at hand.*
*I smell only from afar*
*the scent of death*
*and the yellow scent of marigolds*
*but I feel nothing at all.*
*Twin currents of inconstant pain*
*flow all around me.*
*Beneath the white shroud of a memory on the wane*
*I end up missing out*
*on an emptiness.*
*A footpath that never comes to an end.*
*A purplish tear*
*An evening fading into evening*
*The wind brings about a saffron smile*
*opening like a flower.*
*Your brow creased with lines.*
*The prayer descends only during the hour*
*which IS dust unto dust.*
*Perhaps my voice itself is a hindrance.*
*I can't express myself.*

*From One Loneliness to Another*

## *A SONG OF LIGHT*

*He was a star*
*He could hum nothing but a song of light.*

*When was it,*
*the exact moment,*
*that the pale purple season*
*alighted upon the roseate vast reaches of passion?*
*How would anyone know, Hamid?*

*He was like a bird,*
*decked out in feathers bright,*
*up there in a fiery flight,*
*a fire that within him raged.*
*He carried in his wings*
*a silver-lined ardent desire,*
*all afire,*
*to forge a shiny white path through the murky clouds.*

*With his sparkling breath*
*he drew lines*
*on the wind's dark page.*
*He was the glimmering shore of a wayward lake*

*that belonged to a tale of dreams.*
*He was a blossoming emblem*
*it seems*
*of something new*
*softly walking down ancient ways.*
*He was a star.*

*He heard the tremulous sound*
*of playing instruments*
*in the tinkling rain;*
*picking out fresh hues for the days in the offing*
*even from the rainy season that was already over.*

*Perhaps he meant to fashion a butterfly*
*or a rainbow from the dawn-like intonation*
*of his words of prayer.*

*He was a star*
*He could hum nothing but a song of light.*

*(For bhai Irshad Hussain)*

## *BEHIND YOUR SHAWL'S HEM*

*You know, mother*
*there were not many toys*
*to play with in those days?*

*It was just one of your gentle smiles*
*which cast over my childhood*
*a golden glow,*
*while I played on and on. I don't know why,*
*but I feel as if*
*I still walk through the bazaar of time*
*holding on to your finger.*

*Hiding behind your shawl's hem*
*-a dream shawl-*
*I stare at life as it changes from moment to moment.*
*I blink my eyes in astonishment.*
*I still feel…*

*(For my loving mother)*

## *BEYOND THE SHORE OF TWILIGHT*

*The prayers that are said for you*
*are like margins marking*
*the wreath of fresh flowers.*

*The vines of fortitude and restraint*
*enclose your grave.*
*Somewhere beyond the time*
*measured in months and years*
*the flowers of an everlasting spring bloom*
*and spread their fragrance in the air.*

*The advent of autumn*
*can never spoil their freshness.*

*The shadow of a cloud of certitude*
*lies over the sunlight*
*of what is probable.*
*We have lost our eyes*
*somewhere in the course of our journey*
*but the stars clink in the wind's fist.*

*The faded wounds smoulder anew like destinations.*

*From One Loneliness to Another*

*The elegance of memories alights on the burning sands.*

*Beyond the shore of twilight's grace,*
*held in the evening's arms,*
*the call to prayers,*
*like the glad tidings*
*of a dawn in the offing,*
*sweeps onward.*

*(In the loving memory of my father)*

## IN A DENSELY DEEP NIGHT

*We go along*
*in a densely deep night*
*humming a song.*
*A purplish grey cloud overhead*
*and clouds which look as if*
*coated with clay.*
*Lost moments define the time gone astray.*
*Metaphors of a dwindling winter*
*which hint at seclusion and sadness.*
*The back issue of Funoon,*
*Lakshmi Chowk, the Mall,*
*the Lawrence Garden, the Pak Tea House.*
*Everywhere*
*the ghazals of Khalid Ahmad are being discussed,*
*arguments that go on and on.*

*The journalists lay bare the benighted news.*
*The soldiers deliver fresh messages.*
*Are these just words?*
*A jitteriness or what?*

*He says in a deeply mournful voice:*

*From One Loneliness to Another*

*"Perhaps it is not even a divine decree."*

*The wind battles with the trees and stares at the stars*

*as they make their moves*

*marking each one out.*

*Suddenly the brilliant tones of Mehdi Hasan swirl in the air.*

*On the footpath*

*a handful of moths clinging to a pale light*

*make rhyming patterns.*

*An auto rickshaw, exhausted by its daylong run,*

*goes on muttering to itself.*

*Smoke?*

*A line or verse?*

*A lullaby?*

*Again, the same played-out chatting.*

*Again, the same unreal faces.*

*Again, the same distorted messages.*

*Facebook, Instagram, Twitter, YouTube*

*And far off, swinging from a lamp post,*

*a discoloured sign, perhaps in Urdu.*

*Smoking...? No smoking?*

*The paper kites entangled*

*From One Loneliness to Another*

*in the electricity wires.*
*In Yaqoo' s café sinuous steam rises*
*from tea which is as turbid as the night itself,*
*clings to a tweeting table and stares*
*at the crowded pages of a newspaper.*
*The sun will also come up*
*from behind the clinking cups*
*to seek out the blue butterflies draped in satin.*

*My friends,*
*hold on a little, hold on.*
*Come, let us tickle again*
*the days*
*which have turned away from us,*
*as we go along,*
*in a densely deep night,*
*humming a song.*

*(In the loving memory of Khalid Ahmad)*

## ON THE BLANK EVENING'S PAGE

*Things look so peculiar today.*
*What's gone wrong*
*with the scenic sky over the Mall?*
*No hustle and bustle at all.*
*There is nothing but total*
*stillness all around.*
*The air full of stifled sobs.*
*Almost a drab ambience,*
*as if Sadequain*
*has written in a light blue shade*
*on the evening's blank page*
*the word 'Farewell'.*

## *STREET 40*

*(A poem from my childhood)*

*Just now all of us were here,*
*playing hide and seek and singing:*
*"Come hide, lie low.*
*Sweet corn is ripe.*
*The princess comes in tow."*
*Your voice echoes through the faintly pale*
*hall of the evening;*
*or perhaps I merely intuit that I have heard*
*the echo of your voice.*
*With great difficulty*
*I manage to hide myself behind a grimy door.*
*And how easily you track me down.*
*Yes, it is my turn now.*
*Suddenly the evening's gloom intensifies.*
*I call you by your name*
*from the porch where it is so damp.*

*Behind which window's frame you hide,*
*while the dark adheres to the crazy windows,*
*somewhere in the disjointed shadow of the derelict*
*house?*

*From One Loneliness to Another*

*All my playmates make their way home.*
*A nameless fear begins to rattle me.*
*I say: "Come, let us put an end to this game now."*
*And then I stare upwards where,*
*far away, from the sky,*
*and far away, from the high*
*bough of the red twilight,*
*pale purple leaves,*
*like a spent life,*
*come swirling down.*
*The corners of the sky*
*are blurred by the darkness.*
*The night descends like a haze.*
*Even the fear of being alone*
*seems a little sleepy.*

## *THE SAME CLUSTER OF BREATHS*

*Recognition, perhaps half lost,*

*let's itself be glimpsed*

*in the juxtaposition of words,*

*a reluctance garbed in yellowish-brown.*

*The house's courtyard is suffused*

*with October's damp daylight.*

*Thereafter, from Lahore to Dhaka*

*a wheezy, soiled*

*and bedraggled breeze*

*takes on the appearance of memories.*

*Bright water lies*

*on each side.*

*The obsolete clink of the coins*

*which belong to the past*

*slips through the decrepit grasp of time.*

*The pen inscribes rage*

*across the silence of the page.*

*The wild growth of words*

*From One Loneliness to Another*

*even now lie entangled*

*in the hedge*

*which has been carefully trimmed.*

*(For Jahidul-Haq; a poet friend from Bangladesh)*

## AN EVENING STROLL

*A gust of dreams and fragrance*
*swept across my senses*
*like a passing shower.*
*Whom did I recall once more?*
*Reflections accumulate*
*still more reflections.*
*The rain fan out*
*in all directions.*
*The lanes stretch forth*
*like a parade of mirrors.*
*The evening stroll*
*won over my heart.*

# THE RAINBOW

*It keeps on raining*
*and the rains disappear*
*within rains.*
*The words blend*
*with other words.*
*The roadways*
*jumble up.*
*Silken fancies, roses*
*and sweet smells.*
*A dazzling idea,*
*a dream of growth.*
*On the heavenly shawl*
*of the sunlight*
*stretches out*
*the colorful rainbow*
*of life.*

# *Reviews*

*From One Loneliness to Another*

*From One Loneliness to Another*

# A Journey Through Hidden Worlds ...!

## Bismillah-ir-Rahman-ir-Rahim

Syed Hamid Yazdani's "From One Loneliness to Another" is a journey through hidden worlds that exist in plain sight, memories amidst enchanted surroundings. With their sidewalks and city streets to waterfronts and lonely cafes, the days, nights and seasons arrive and form the sceneries that frame each poem. It's these happenings around us (and even within us) that mark the elusive passage of time. They continue uninterrupted, often without our awareness.

Here, however, the poet's focused perception and vivid descriptions bring these telling backdrops to the forefront. A masterful use of metaphors and personification reveal the palpable surrealness within each time and place. In each setting, the reader suddenly finds themselves alienated from the superficial. These detached liberating moments of awareness catch the significance of various metaphors, symbols and signposts even amidst their constant flux. Flipping through memories, to which place will we be led next and what mysteries there will be uncovered?

We are fortunate for Salim-ur-Rahman saheb whose selection and translation of these poems from their original Urdu has produced such an organic presentation. His vision and efforts have allowed this experience to be shared with English readers.

Finally, congratulations to Syed Hamid Yazdani saheb whose literary contributions continue to reach wider audiences. I look forward to revisiting the times, places and feelings evoked in each of these captivating pages.

*Irshaad Ahmad Rashid*
*Toronto, Canada 202*

## Enchanting Poetry of an Alluring Nostalgia

George Steiner says, "Without translation, we would be living in provinces bordering on silence." There is always a paradox in a translated version; it can be both extraordinarily communicative and extremely elusive but when you come across a work of translation that elevates itself to the status of trans-creation, you feel as if the book was written twice. This is what happened to me while going through my favourite poet Hamid Yazdani's poems rendered into English by Muhammad Salim ur Rahman. Salim sb. is an eminent writer and translator. I am deeply impressed by the way he gives an invisible twist to the original poem through his clever craft.

Reading Hamid Yazdani has always been a treat for me. His poems hold my hand and take me to a wonderland where I keep wandering with my eyes wide open like Alice. While reading his enchanting poetry, I am always lost in the process of being and becoming, the quiet introspection and an alluring nostalgia. Someone makes me take a plunge on the attic of memory and remember the good old days of Government College Lahore when I used to see a blooming young man clad in G.C maroon blazer and coming out of every literary gathering with flying colours.

Listening to your heart may sound too good to be true but I like to lend my ear to its silent steps. I am in love with the soft footsteps of Hamid's poems that take me " On The Ultimate Shore" "During A Squarish Night" and keep telling me through " A Long Distance Call" that "Night Is A Footloose Girl" and share with me "A Dream On The Wings Of Butterfly".

*Salman Basit*
*Professor of English Literature*
*Air University, Islamabad. Pakistan*

## About the Poet
## Hamid Yazdani

Hamid Yazdani appeared on the poetry scene of Pakistan in the eighties. He inherited the art of writing poetry from his father Syed Yazdani Jalandhari who was a famous poet, writer and journalist. Hamid's Urdu and Punjabi poetry books include 'Abhi Ik Khwab Rehta Hai' (1992 & 2008), 'Gehri Sham ki Bailein' (2008), 'Raat Di Neeli Chup' (2002) and 'Ita`at' (2011). His latest book is an Urdu short story collection titled 'Khaali Balti' (2022).

Hamid was born in Lyallpur (now Faisalabad) in 1961 but was raised in the educational and literary environment of Lahore from where he obtained Masters Degree in Sociology from the University of the Punjab. Hamid also has the honour to be a Ravian (a student of prestigious Government College, Lahore). Later on, he received a Master of Social Work (MSW) degree from Wilfred Laurier University, Waterloo, Canada and an Honours Social Services Worker Diploma from Mohawk College, Hamilton.

Hamid now works in the social services sector and lives in Waterdown, Ontario, Canada with his family. He can be reached at hamidyazdani@hotmail.com.

## About the Translator
## Muhammad Salim-ur-Rahman

Salim-ur-Rahman is a respected short story writer, poet, literary editor and translator from Pakistan. He is known for translating both from English to Urdu and vice versa. He translated some of the gems of world literary classics including Homer's The Odyssey, Joseph Conrad's Heart of Darkness, Anton Chekhov's plays Three Sisters and The Seagull, and Yasunari Kawabata's The Sound of the Mountain and Sun Tzu's The Art of war.

He also translated Urdu literature into English. The translation of selected Urdu short stories by him was published under the title of The Naked Hens. His poems, Essays, short stories and articles have also been printed. He used to edit a prestigious Urdu literary journal Savera, as well.

Salim-ur-Rahman, born in 1934, lives in the city of Lahore; the cultural capital of Pakistan.

www.ingramcontent.com/pod-product-compliance
Lightning Source LLC
Chambersburg PA
CBHW071117090426
42736CB00031B/1878